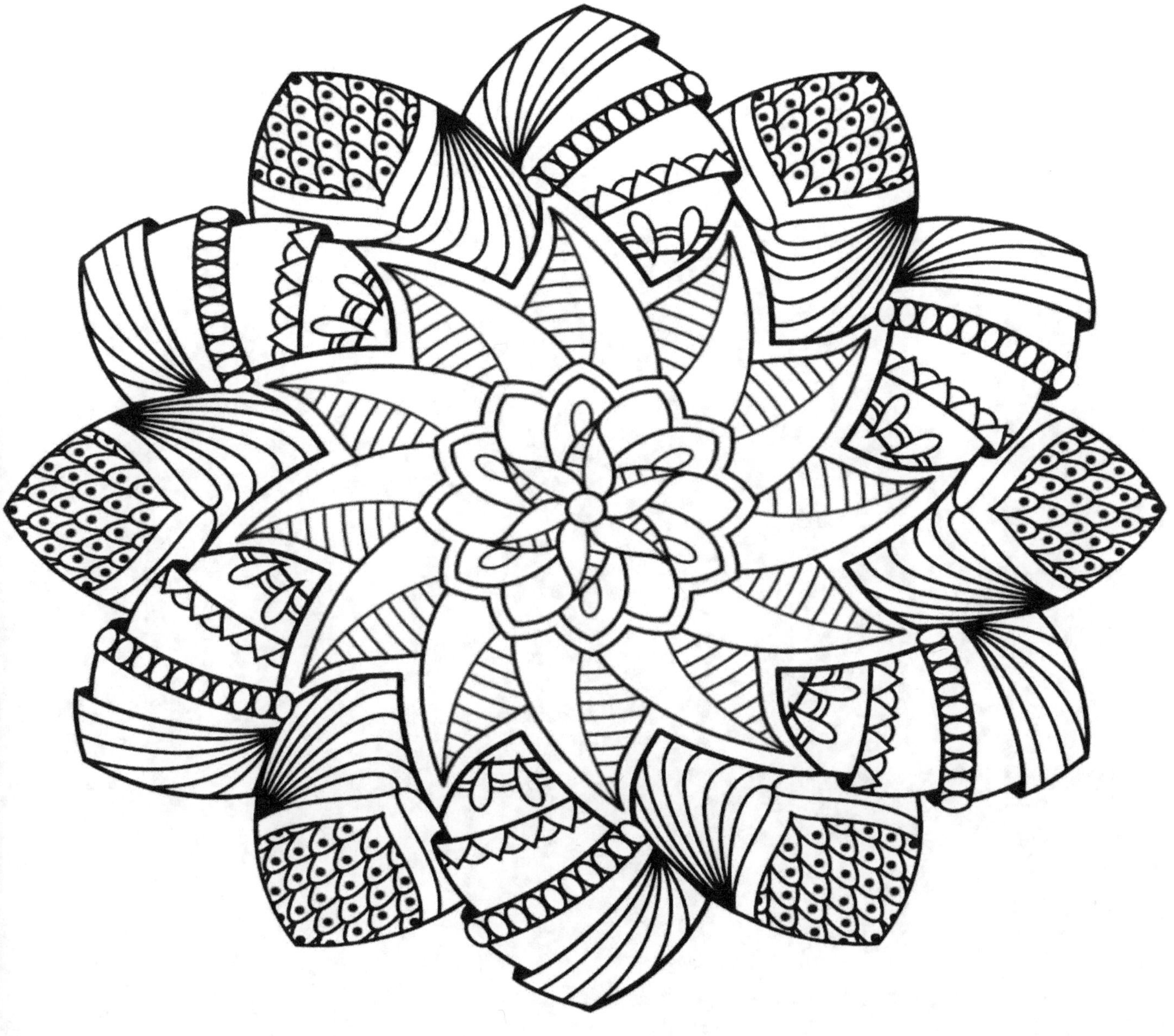

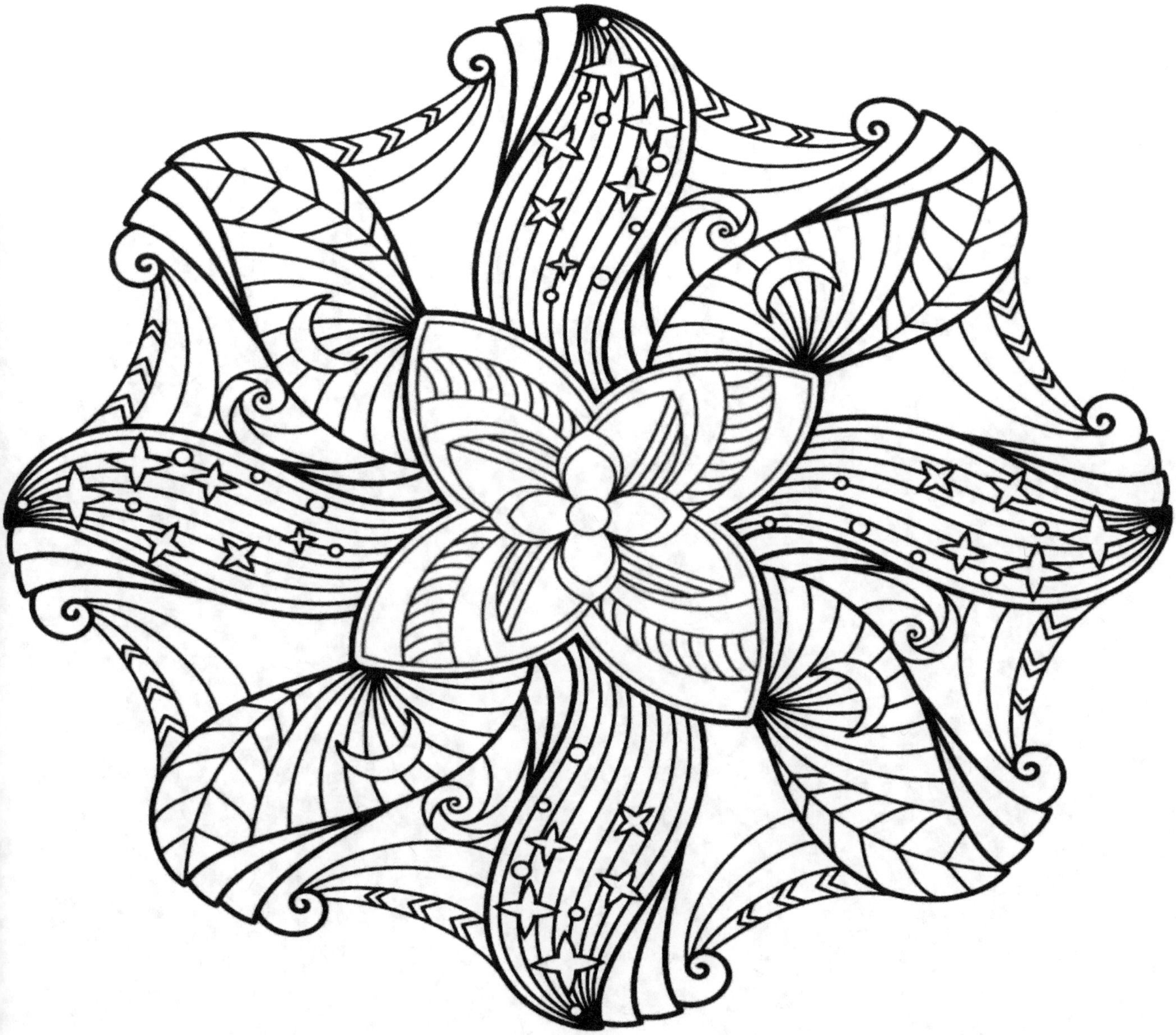

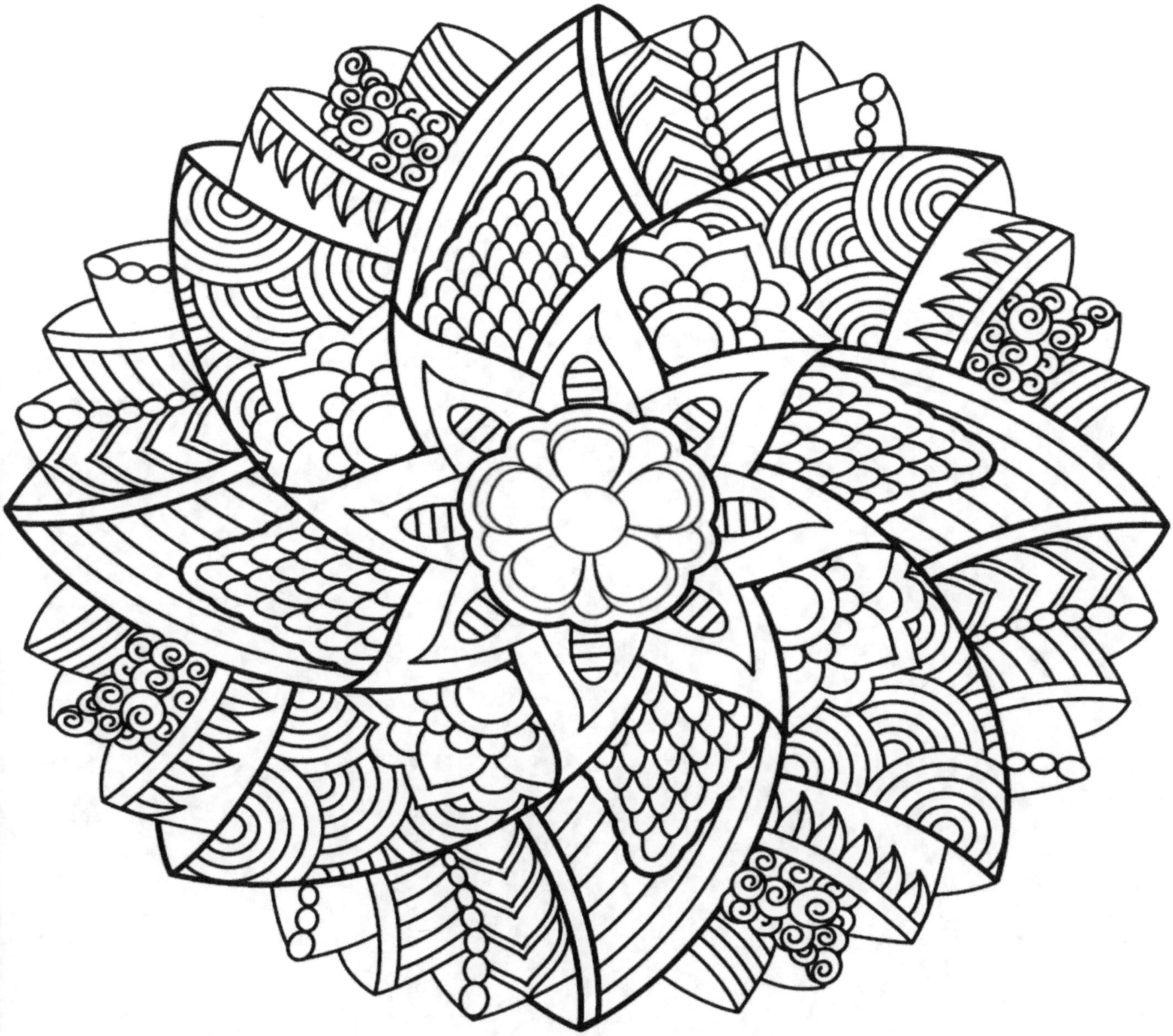

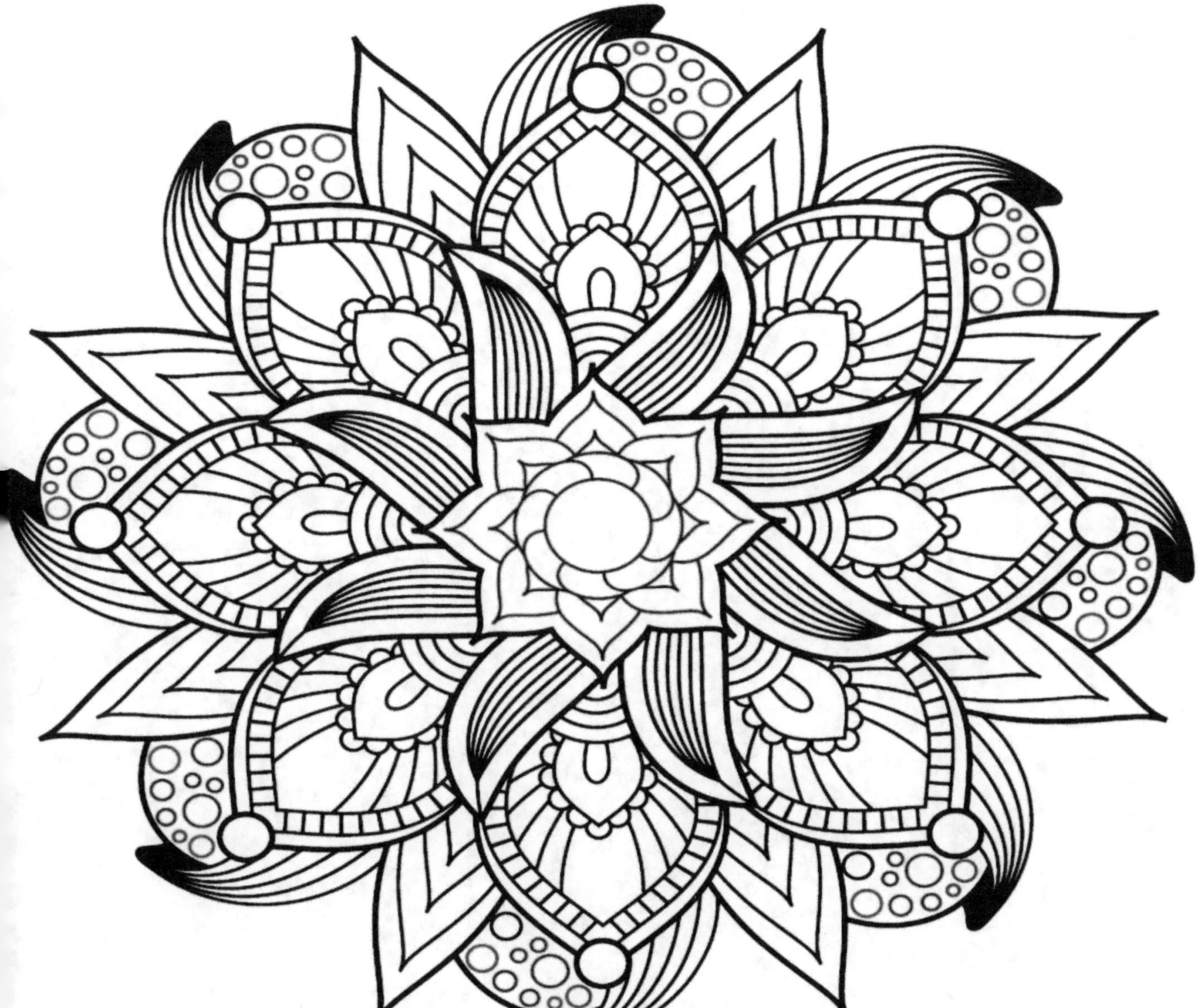

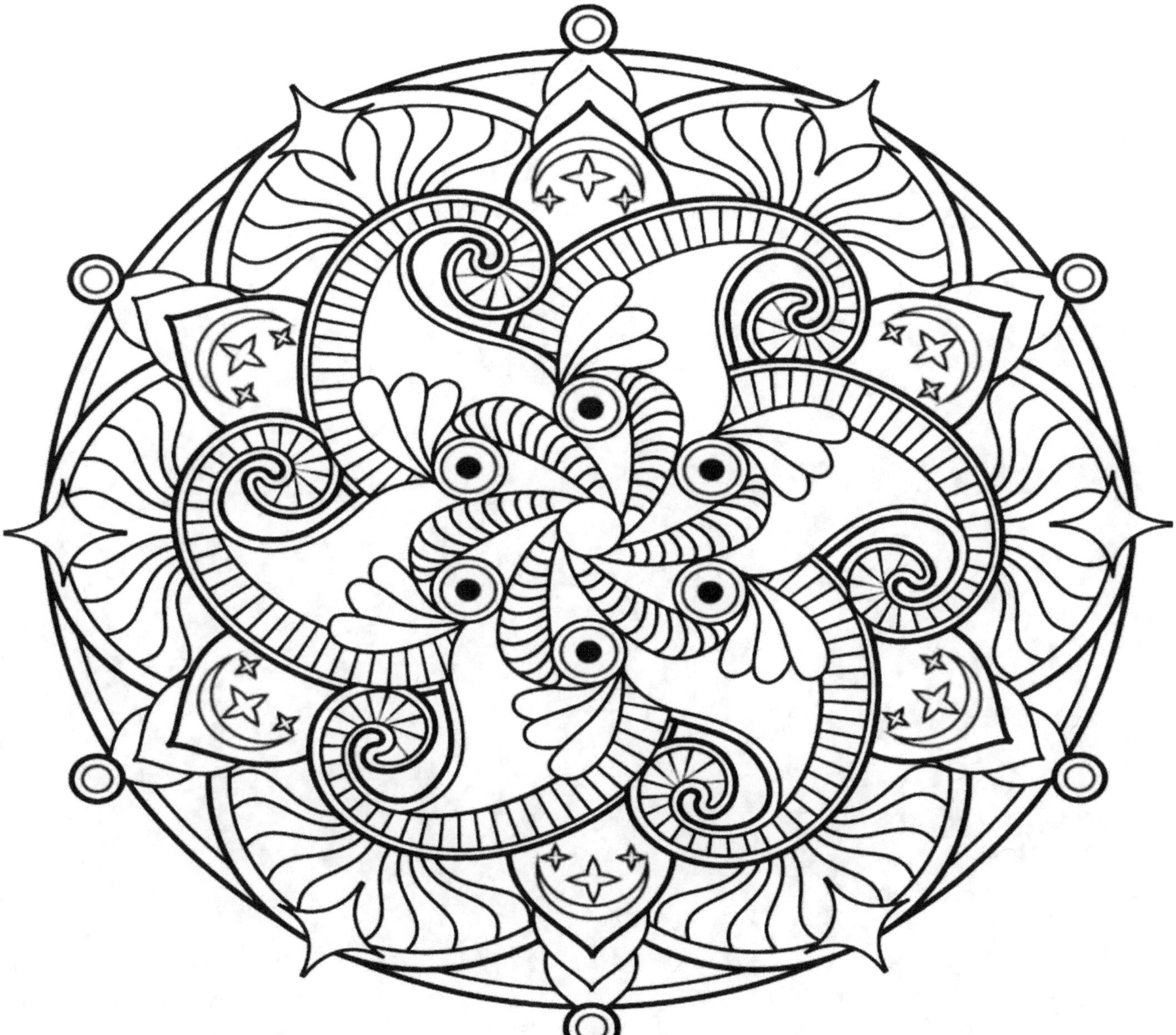

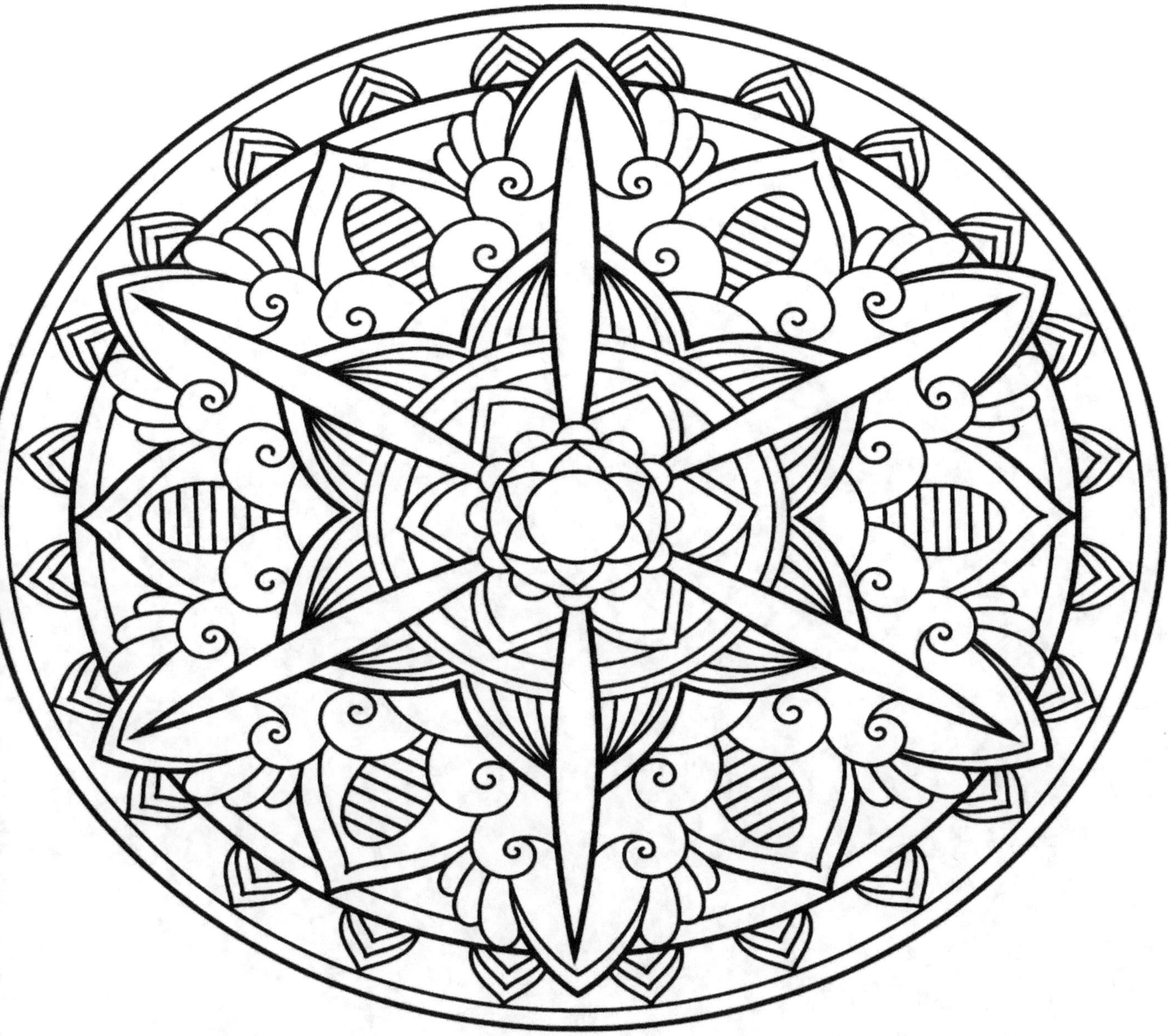

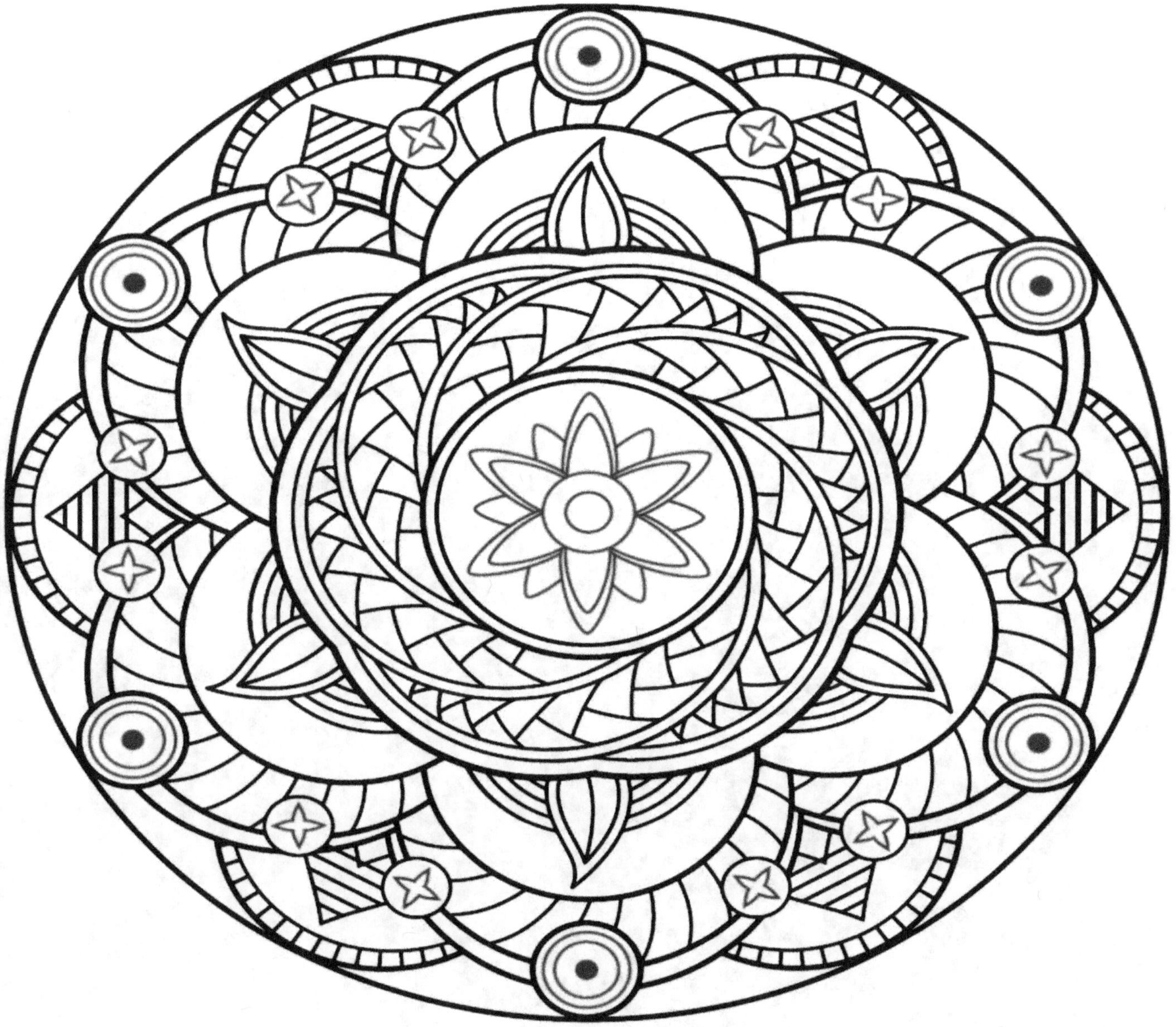

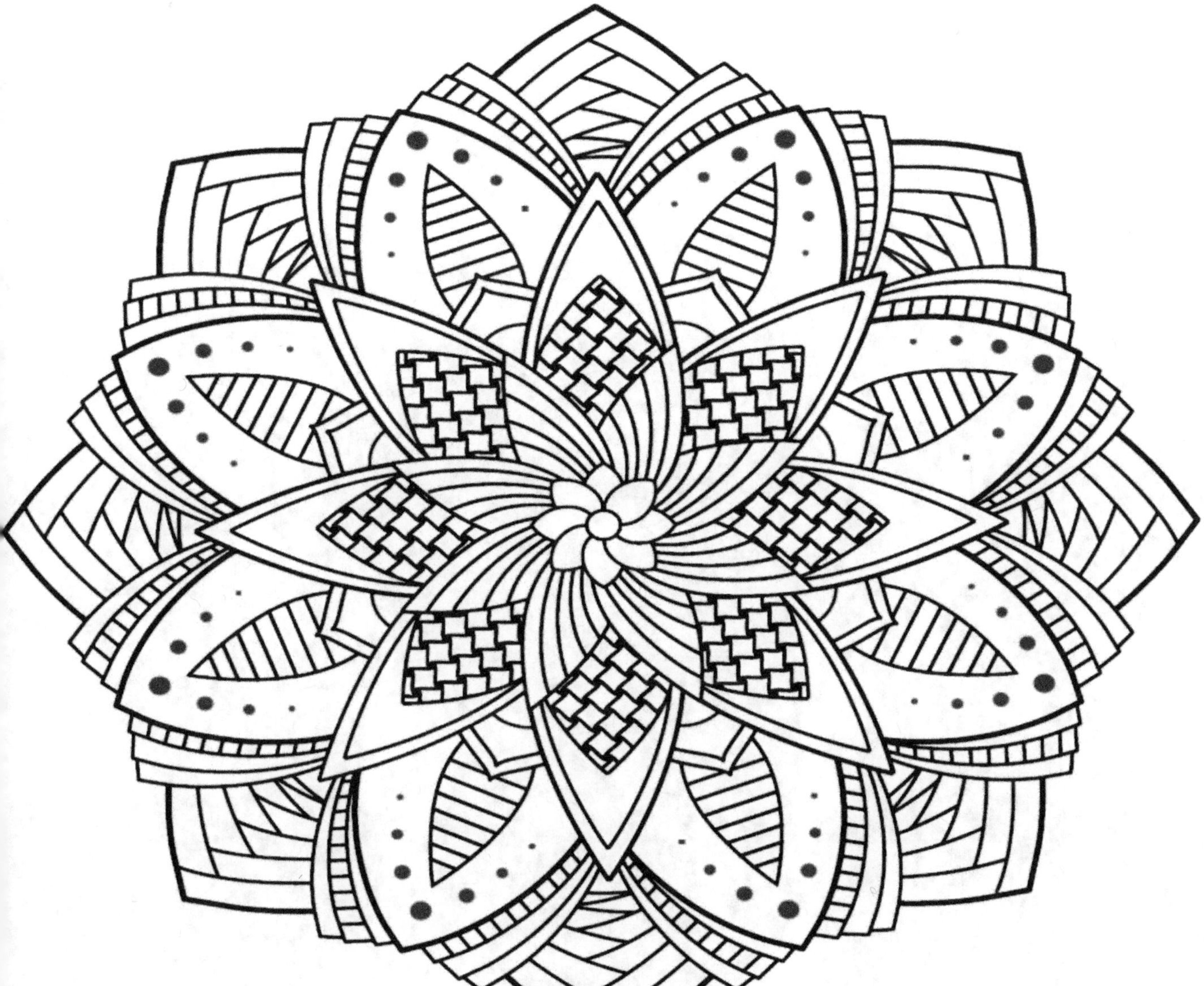

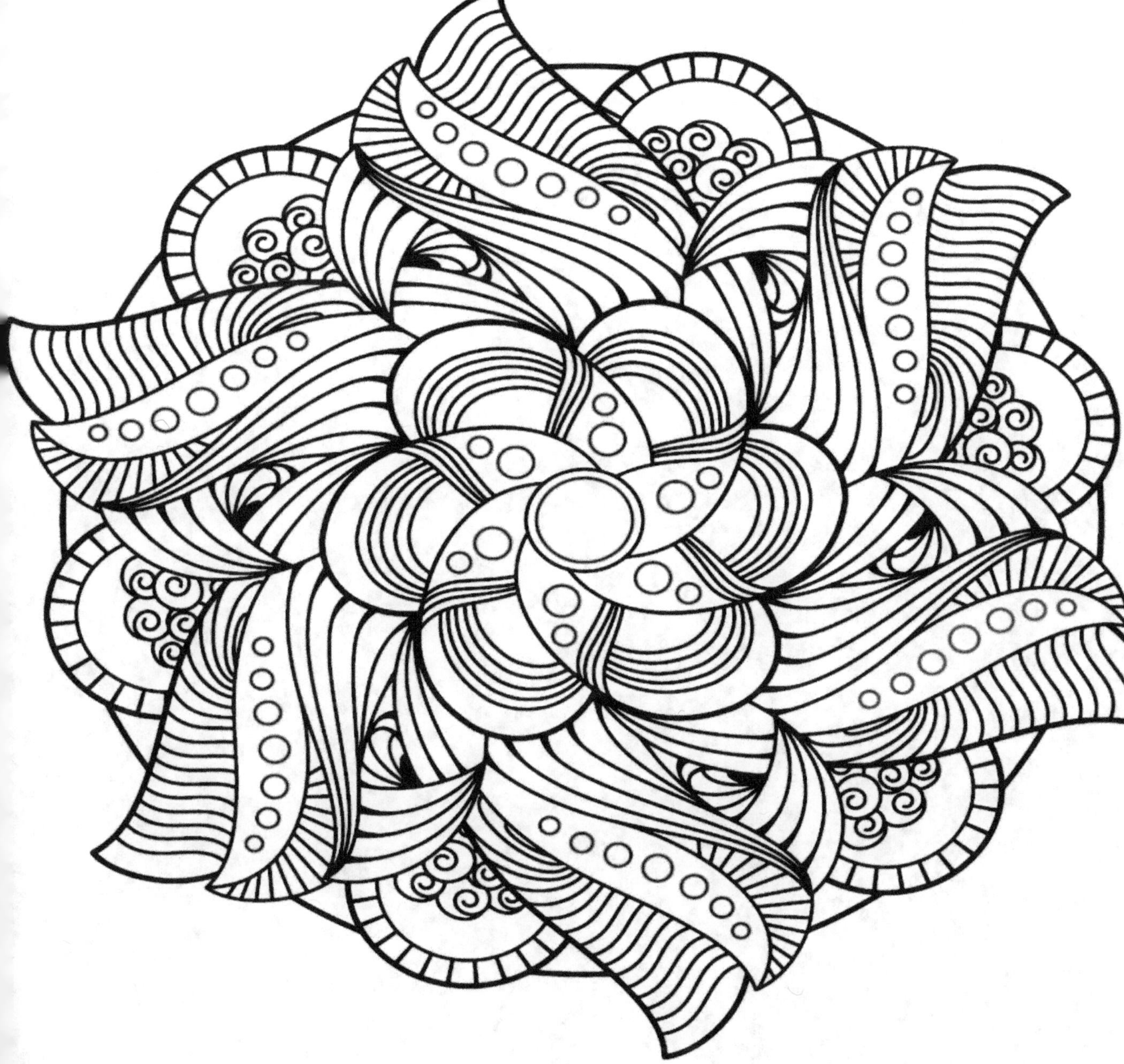

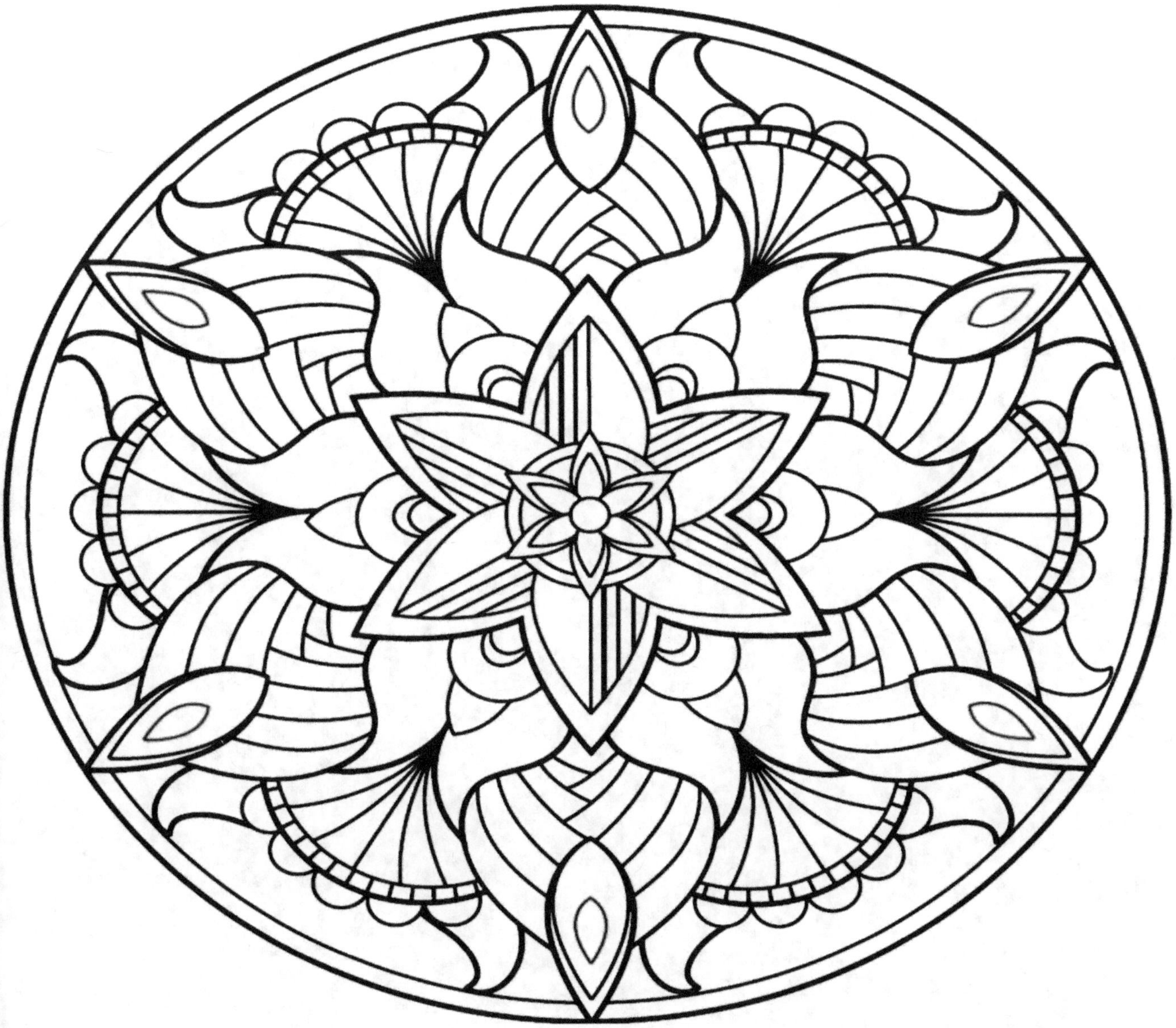

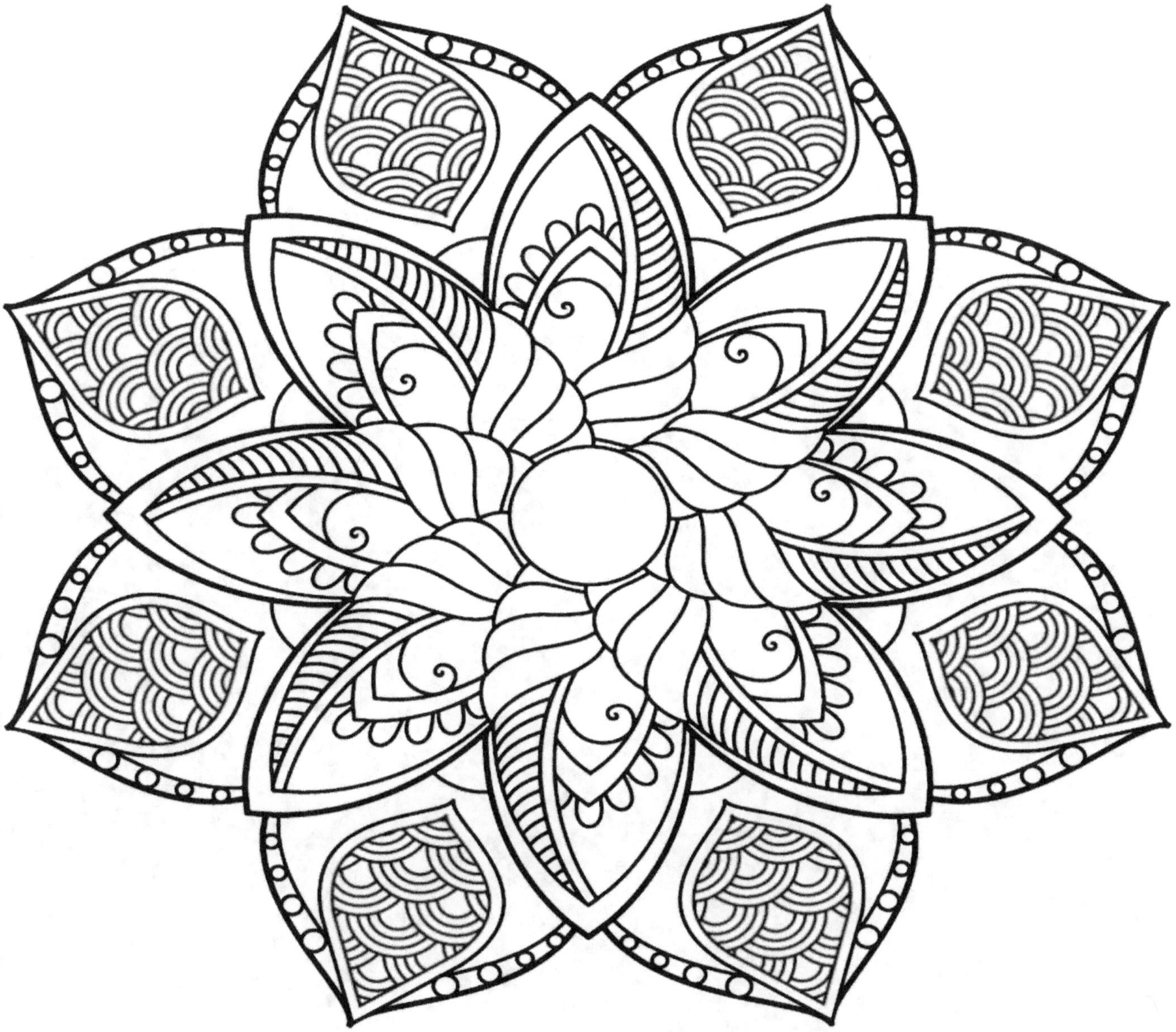

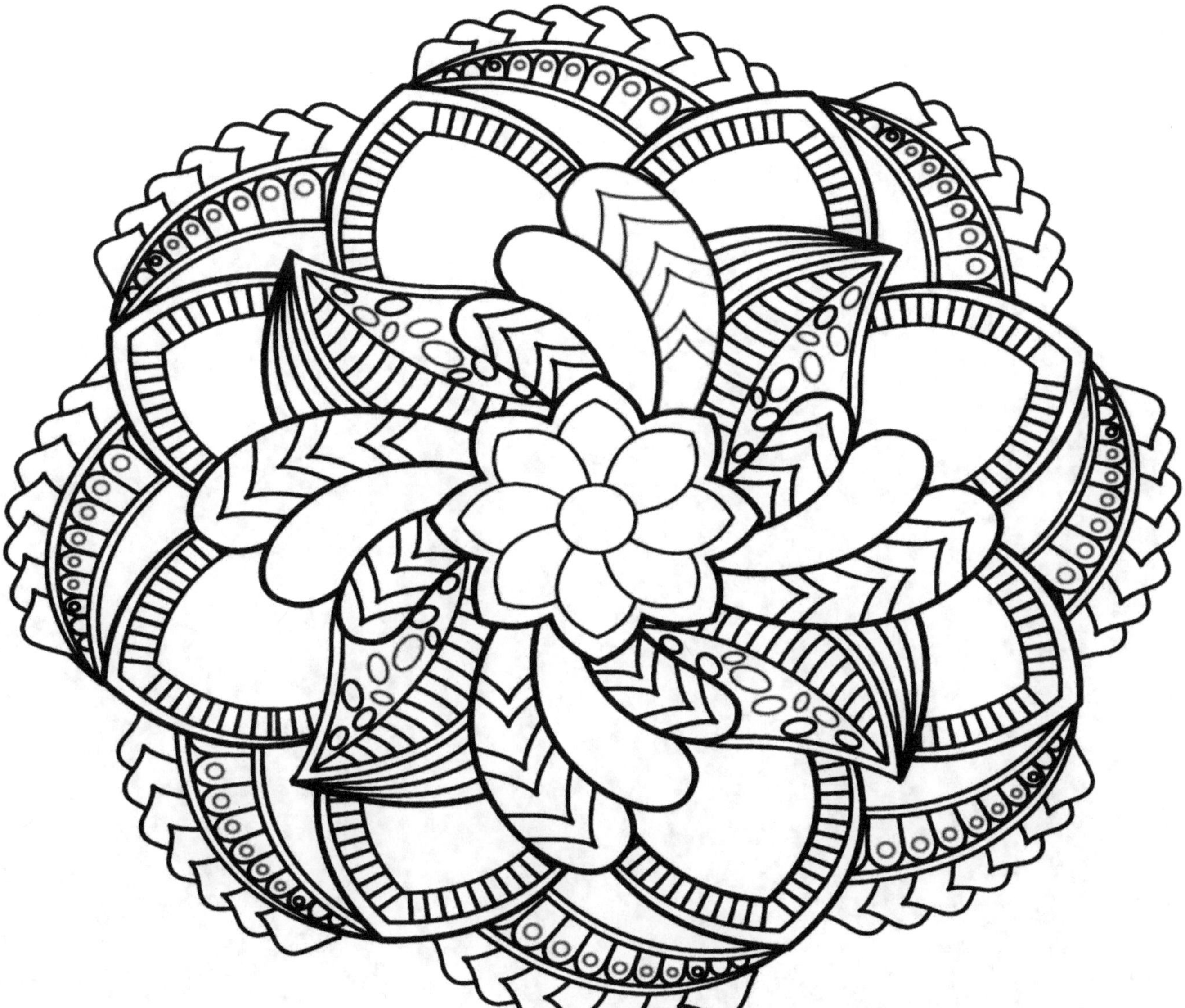

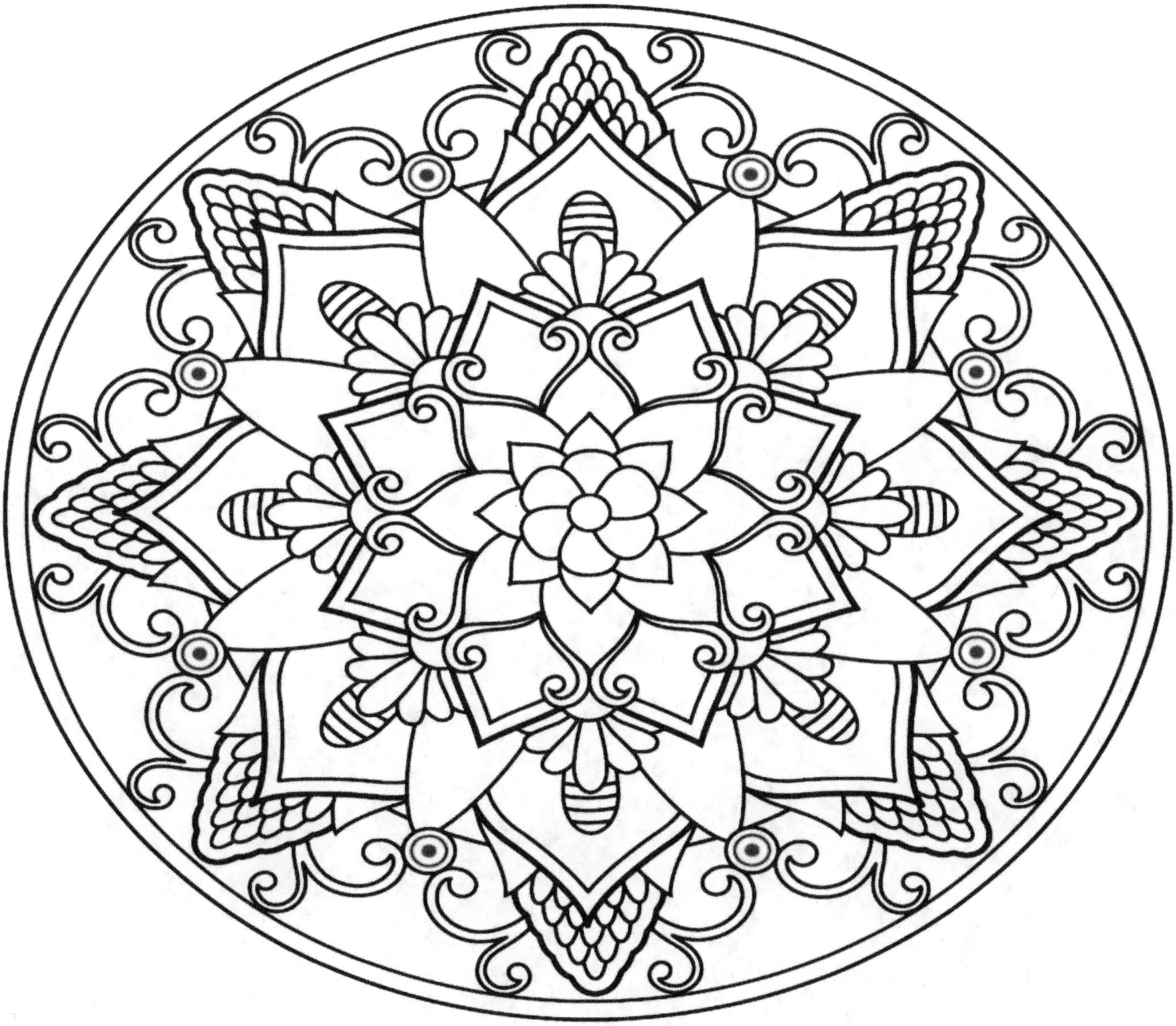

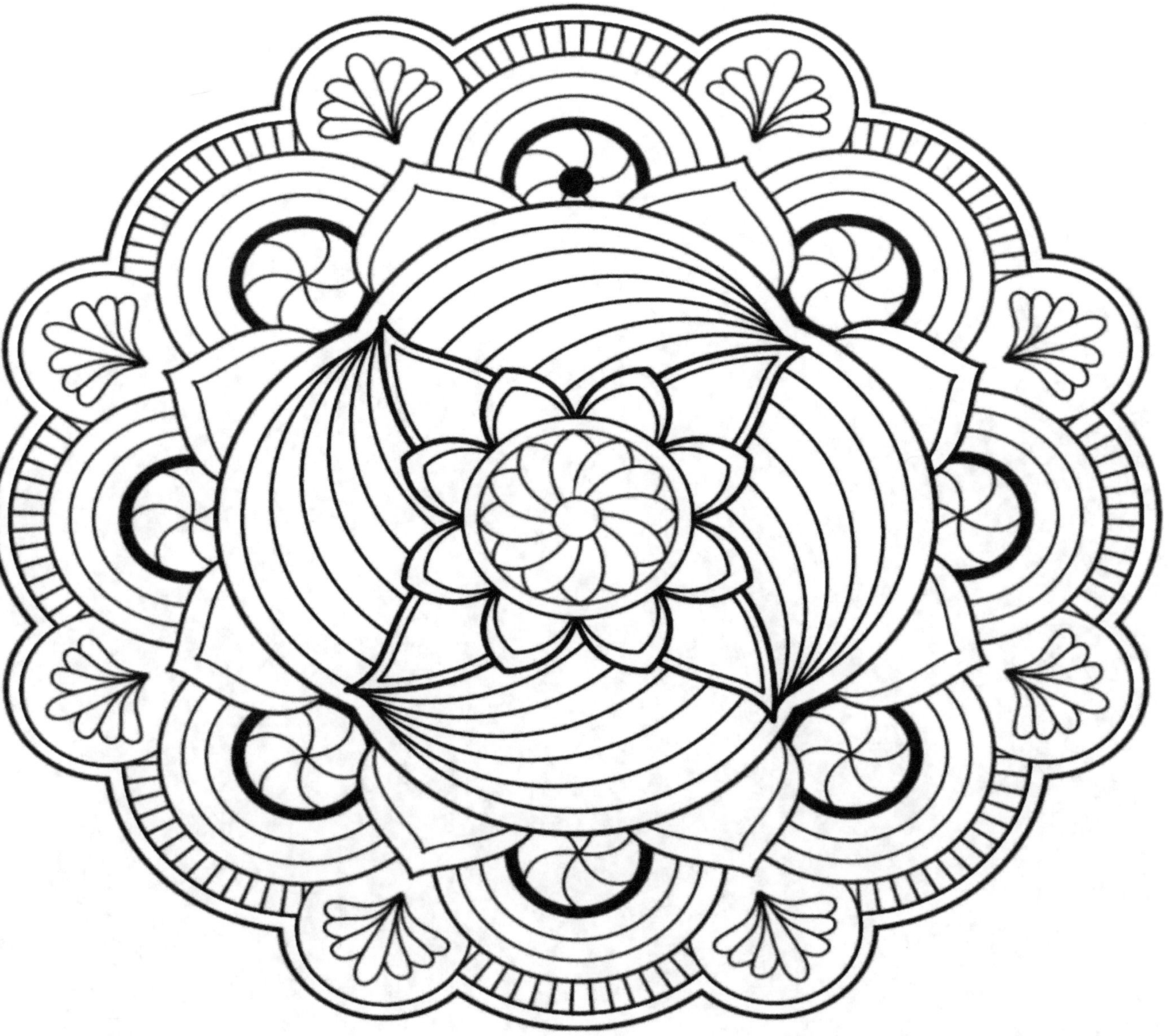

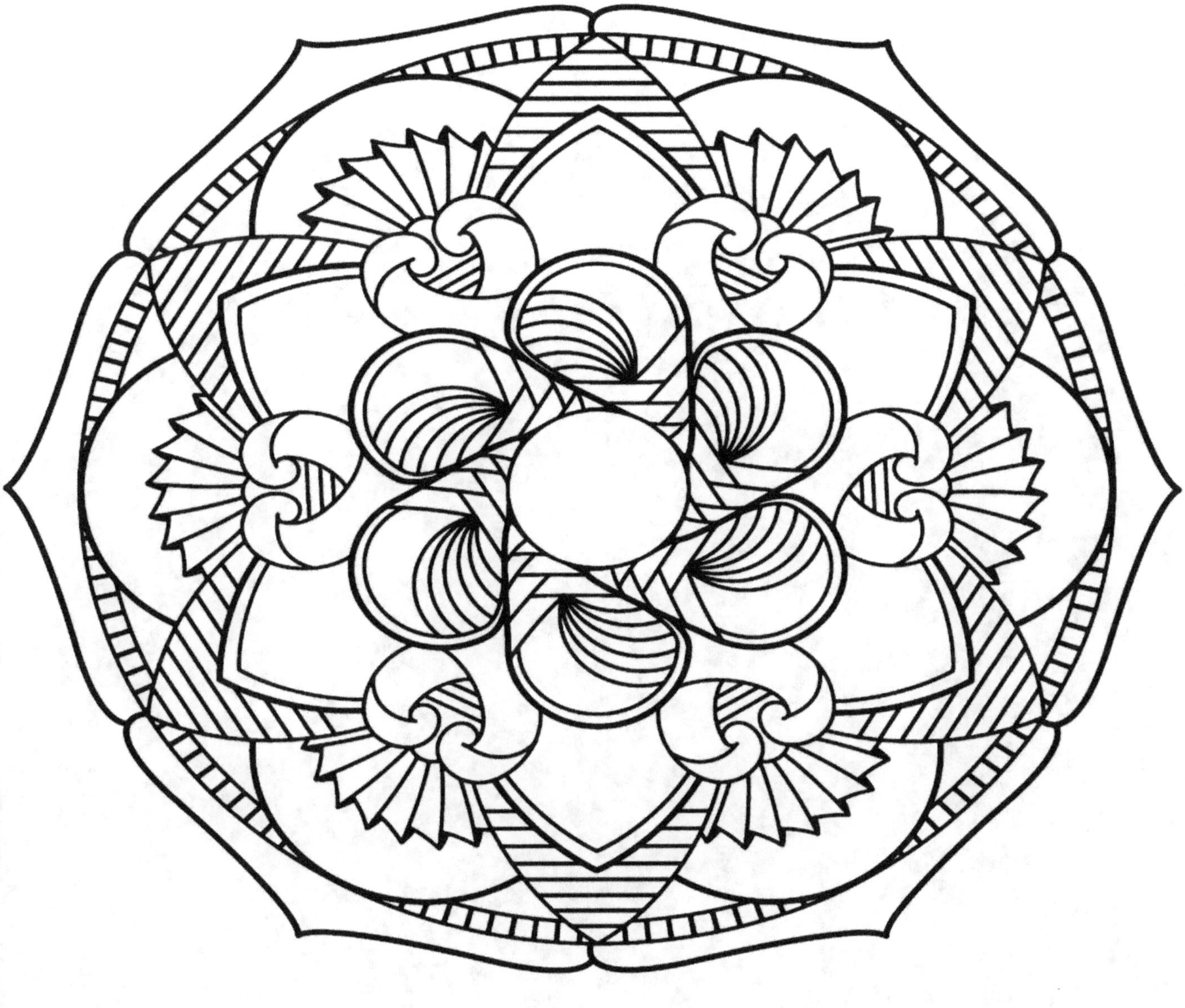

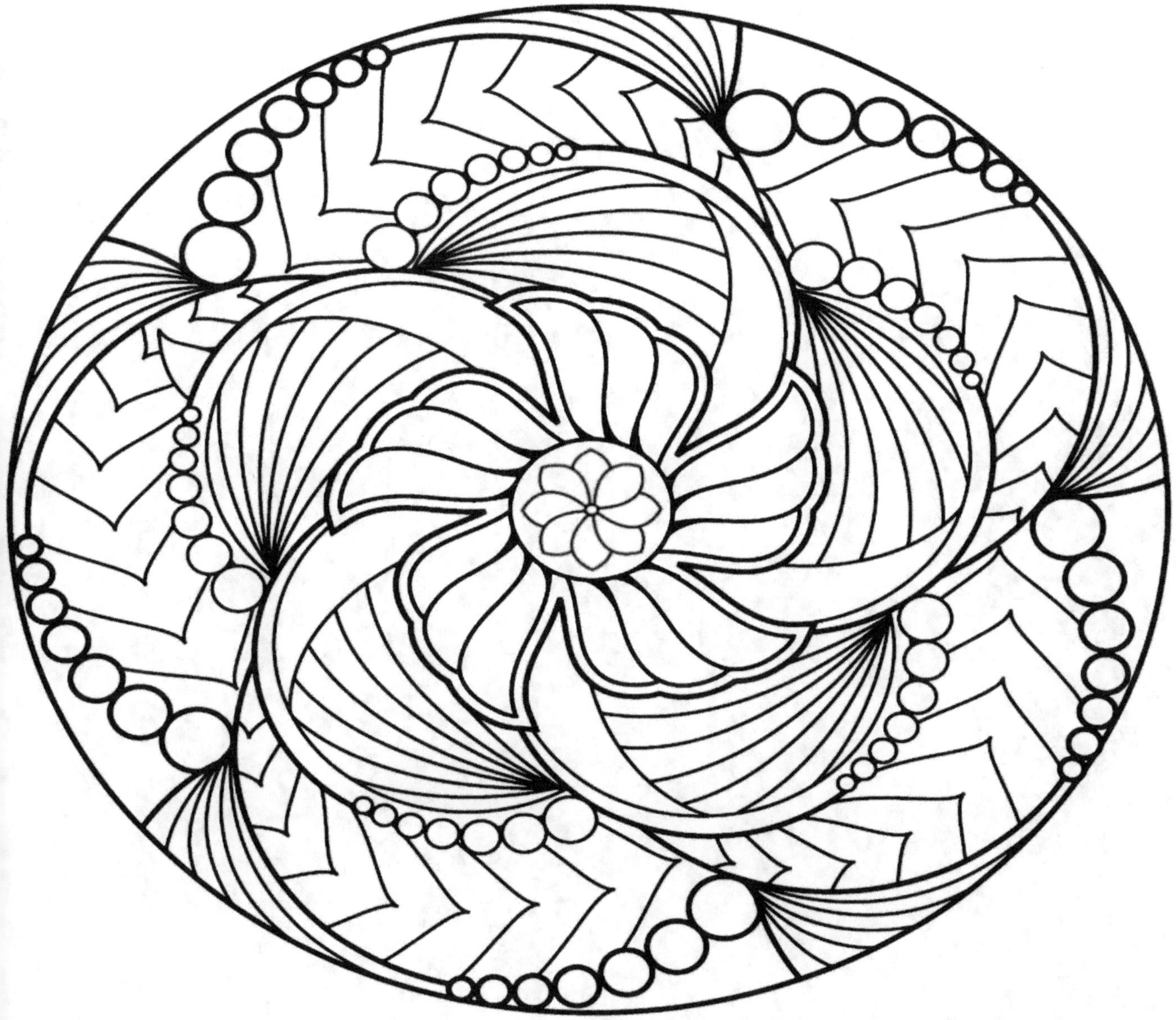

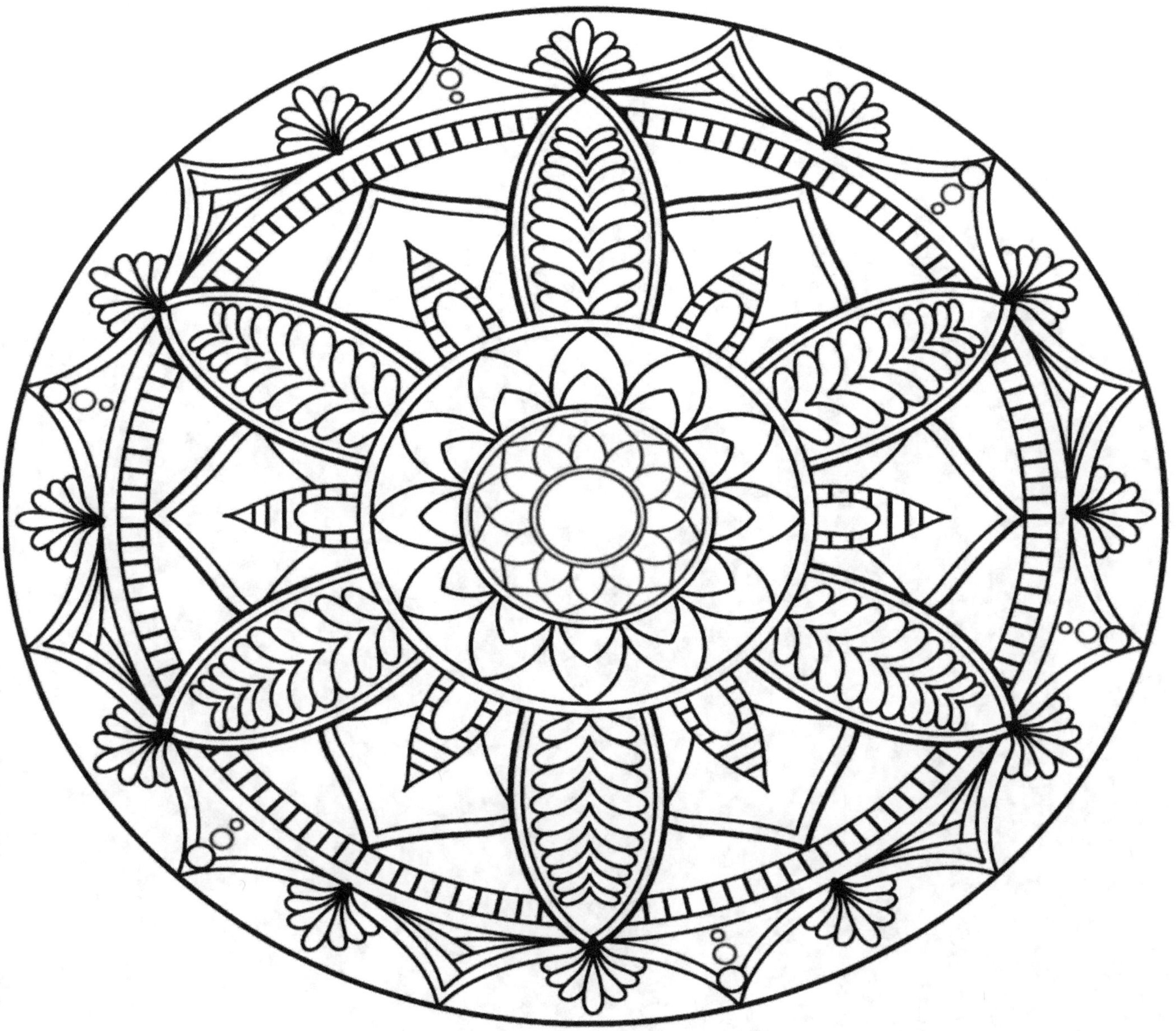

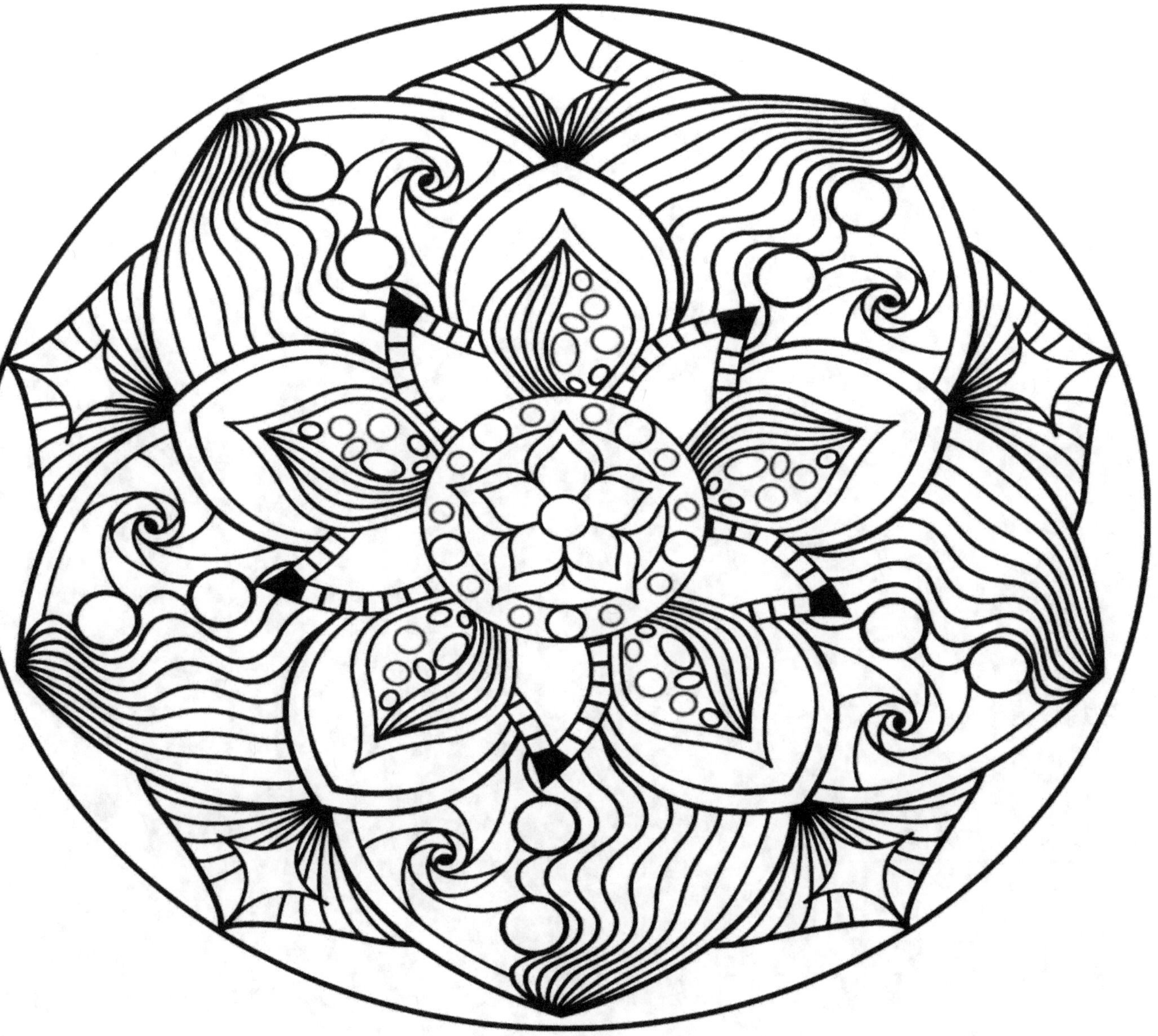

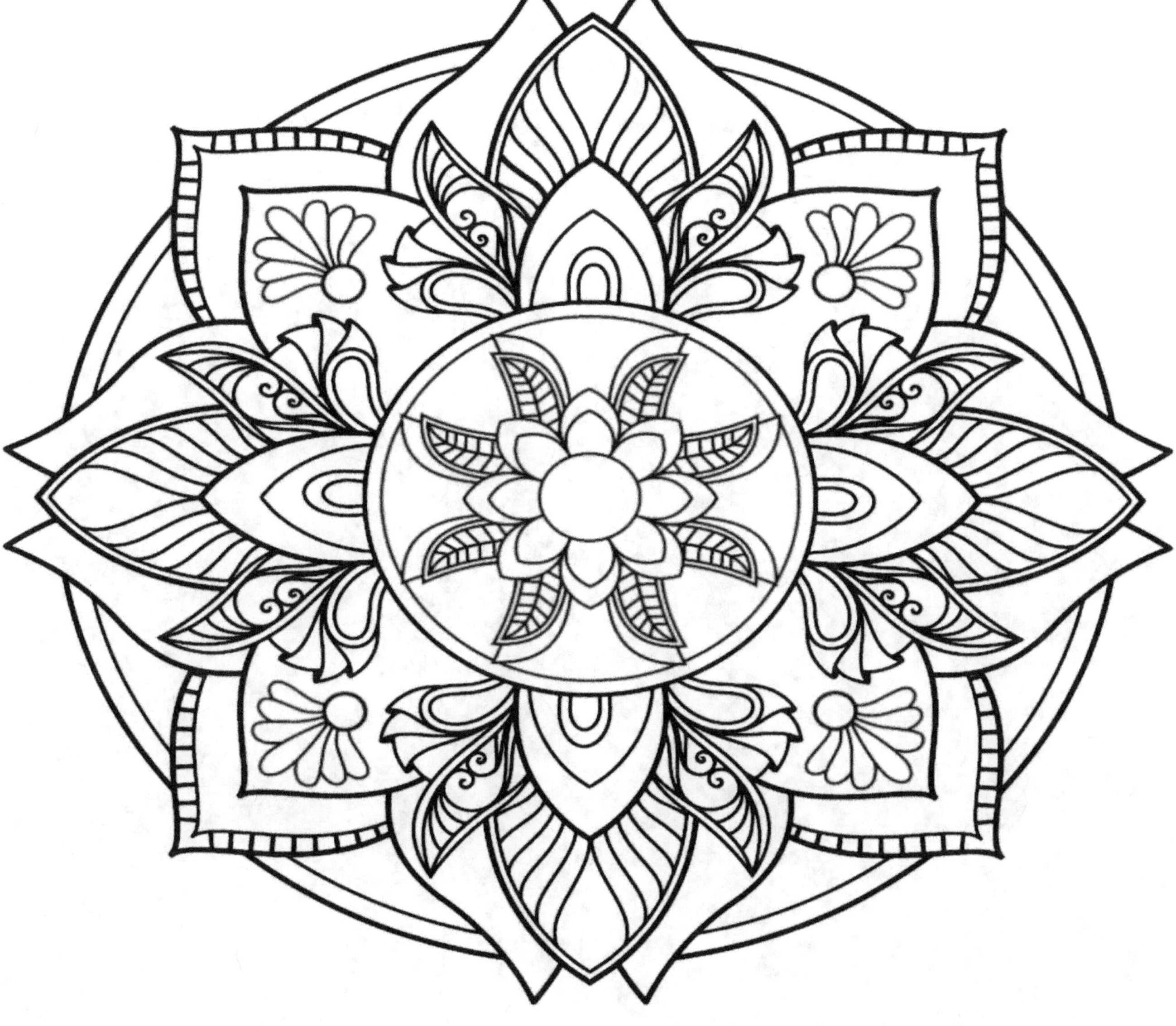

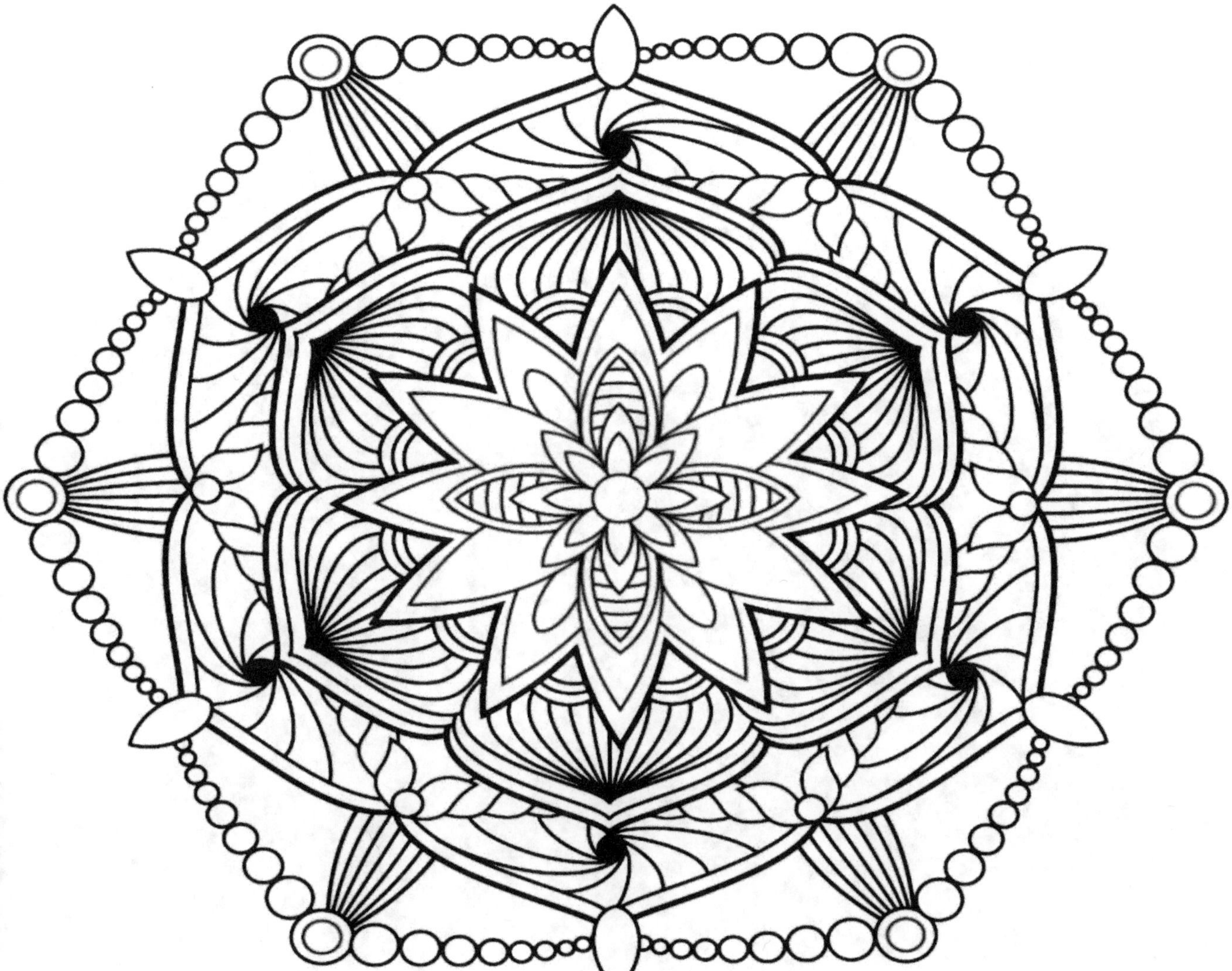

Magic Mandalas Coloring Pages

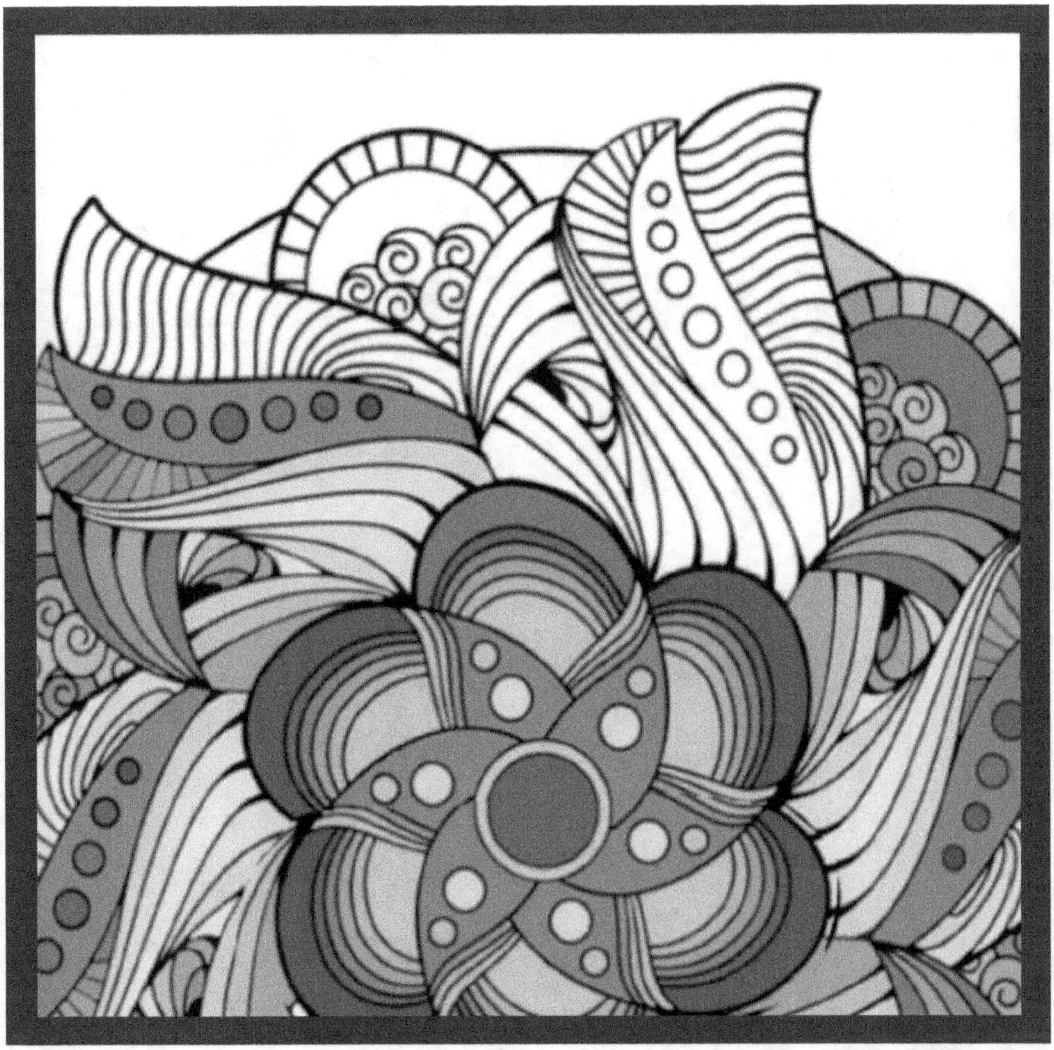